FEATURES

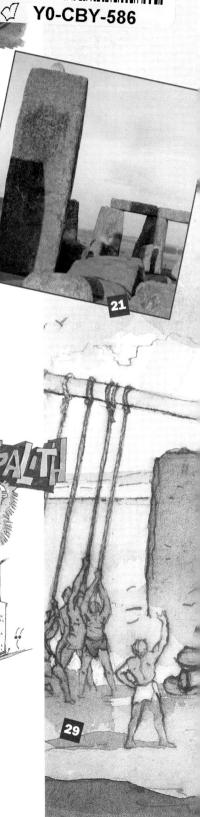

DEPARTMENTS

ACTIVITIES

Musings

The retrieving of these forgotte[n]
resembles the Art of

John Aubrey (1626-1697), English wr[iter]

"Technology" has become one of the most commonly used words in today's world. Companies use it to promote new products in their advertising; scientists use it to explain new theories and inventions; doctors use it to refer to breakthroughs in medical treatments. In fact, technological advances have come to mean progress, with people attaining a higher degree of civilization. There are very few individuals who would eagerly exchange places with an ancient person, since most people consider the ancient way of life less pleasant, even inferior, to their own. Is this true? Or, is this a thought common to every generation's way of thinking?

By definition, technology is "a system by which a specific technical problem is handled." Therefore, as a word, it may refer to methods developed to solve a particular scientific, mechanical, or commercial problem by any people in any time period. Every generation then may be regarded as a stepping stone in technology — that is, the technological advances of each generation serve as a foundation for future advances.

In this issue, we travel back in time to ancient England and a place called Stonehenge, whose builders left no written records to explain how or why they set up a series of giant stones. Through the years, investigators at the site have proposed various theories to explain the "mystery" of the huge blocks, but the questions remain — both about the stones and about the people who erected them.

Nor is Stonehenge the only circle of gigantic stones in Great Britain. There are hundreds of similar circles, including those at nearby Avebury, at Castlerigg in Cumbria, and at Stenness in Orkney. Let's go now and join researchers at Stonehenge as they seek to uncover more about the site and a people who worked with "modern technology" and were the "advanced" generation of their time.

As at Stonehenge, the builders of this burial chamber of Pentre Ifan in the Preseli Mountains area of Wales also used massive "bluestones."

by Glenna Dunning

Imagine that it is just before dawn, 4,000 years ago. You are standing in the middle of Stonehenge, looking east toward the **Heel Stone**, a tall rock located outside the circle. You are waiting for sunrise and, suddenly, there it is! The disk of the sun rises directly over the top of the Heel Stone, indicating an important sign: the summer solstice, the first day of summer and the longest day of the year (on or around June 21).

Why would symbols like this be important to the early people of Britain? Rituals, ceremonies, and agricultural events (like the best time to plant and harvest) took place during specific times of the year, so priests and farmers needed to keep track of those dates. They did not have clocks or written calendars but, if they used Stonehenge as an astronomical observatory as some theories suggest, they could create a simple calendar to mark the passage of time. For example, lining up the paths of the sun and the moon through the sky with various stones and markers could indicate the passing of a month or a year, or note changes in the seasons.

If we look at how Stonehenge is arranged, we can see that it was basically

Legend says a natural round impression on the surface of the so-called **Heel Stone** is the heel print of a monk, at whom the devil threw the stone.

"An ⬥Observa

From the air, Stonehenge's circular formation is much easier to see, especially the outline of the great ditch that originally encircled the monument. Look on pages 6 and 7 for a detailed diagram of the site.

ORY in STONE"

a series of circles with some additional "marker" stones. These stones ran in straight lines from different parts of the circles. The outermost circle has 56 holes (called Aubrey Holes after John Aubrey, who discovered them in the 1666). Then there are two inner circles, one with 30 stones and the other with 29 stones, numbers which may have counted the days of the months. Outside of the circles and located to the northeast is the Heel Stone, and it is the relationship between this large rock and the position of the circles that is the basis for suggesting Stonehenge was an astronomical observatory.

Evidence suggests that the site was built with its main **axis** pointing toward the Heel Stone, which pinpointed sunrise on the first day of summer. This is one of the few facts upon which most scientists and historians agree. There have been other theories as well, such as the suggestion that the winter solstice, the first day of winter and the shortest day of the year, could be predicted by aligning certain stones with the setting of the sun. Another idea is that the 56 Aubrey Holes could predict lunar eclipses. This theory proposes that, immediately after a lunar eclipse, you place a marker in one hole and leave it there for three years, at which time you move it to the next hole and leave it there for three years, and so on. By the time you have moved around the entire circle (about 168 years!), there would be another lunar eclipse.

We will probably never know for certain whether these theories about Stonehenge are right or wrong, because the original builders left no instructions for its use. Some archaeologists reject the idea that the site was ever an observatory and argue that it was intended for religious purposes only. They assume that there was no technologically advanced culture in Britain when Stonehenge was built. Other scientists claim that Stonehenge was built with impressive technical skills and mathematical sophistication.

Heel Stone

Aubrey Holes

While surveying the site, John Aubrey noticed a series of hollow areas that formed a circle inside the ditch surrounding the great stones. The 56 holes were later named after him.

In an effort to discover more about Stonehenge, many scientific studies have been made. In 1740, William Stukeley examined the site and announced that it was "astronomically aligned" toward the summer solstice. In the late 1800s, the celebrated English scientist Sir Joseph Lockyer investigated Stonehenge and declared that it could be used to predict "certain astronomical events."

In 1963, Gerald Hawkins, an American-based astronomer, used a computer to calculate the relationship between the path of the sun and the moon and the layout of various markers, holes, and stones. He announced that the rising and setting of the sun and moon could be predicted accurately, and that the 56 Aubrey Holes could be used to calculate eclipses of the moon. He called Stonehenge a "complicated computer for predicting lunar and solar eclipses," but his findings are controversial within the scientific community.

Today, there is a new science called "archaeoastronomy," which studies the interaction of astronomy with anthropology (the study of humans), religion, mythology, and archaeology. Perhaps archaeoastronomy will finally answer the riddle of mysterious Stonehenge! 🐾

Glenna Dunning *is a librarian who loves to write about science and history. She visited Stonehenge several years ago, but wasn't there at the right time to see the sun rise behind the Heel Stone!*

William Stukeley:
Archaeologist and Archdruid

by Stephanie Prescott

In this 1800's illustration, Druids gather at Stonehenge to celebrate the midsummer solstice, the longest day of the year. According to the artist, they even draped huge banners over the inner megaliths as part of festivities.

By profession, William Stukeley was an eighteenth-century (1700s) doctor who later became an Anglican minister. His hobby, however, was investigating ancient sites and, as a young man in his twenties, he carried out some highly regarded fieldwork, primarily at Stonehenge and Avebury. Stukeley took very precise measurements and carefully recorded and illustrated his findings. However, Stukeley's claim to archaeological fame — or disgrace — is the connection he proposed between the stones and the Druids. It is a connection which, despite the evidence to the contrary, has persisted since he published *Stonehenge: A Temple Restored to the Druids* in 1740. Stukeley's Druids, however, were not exactly the Druids of history.

The ancient Druids were the learned priests of the Celts, who, most scholars believe, originated in Eastern Europe and slowly made their way west. They reached the British Isles soon after 90 B.C., long after Stonehenge was built. Our knowledge of the Druids comes primarily from early Greek and Roman writers, since the Druids left no written records. The Roman

leader Julius Caesar described the Druids as a powerful class of men who acted not only as priests, but also as judges and teachers. They were the authorities on the nature of the heavens, the earth, and the immortal gods. They also believed in and taught the immortality of the soul, which was, as Caesar noted, a great incentive to bravery in battle. The Roman writer Pliny the Elder traced the term Druid to the Greek *drus* (meaning "oak") and the Indo-European *wid* (meaning "knowledge"). He said the Druids worshipped the oak tree and the mistletoe that grew on it. Caesar referred to Druid worship at "sacred groves" — not stone temples. He also described the huge "wicker man" the Druids built to hold the humans and animals they ritually sacrificed atop a bonfire.

*I*n *Stonehenge: A Temple Restored to the Druids,* Stukeley ignored all accounts of cruelties committed by the Druids. His motives were both patriotic and religious: patriotic because he argued that the "British Druids," not the Romans or the Danes (from Denmark), were the builders of Stonehenge; religious because he believed that these wise and peaceful Druids were actually the "earliest Christians" to arrive in Britain. Stukeley even established a British genealogy going back to Noah and the story of the flood that is found in the Bible. According to Stukeley, the Druids were different from Christians who belonged to the Church of England only because they believed "in a Messiah who was to come" while "we believe in [a Messiah who] is come." Stukeley proudly claimed Stonehenge for

his ancestors and established their unbroken connection to the beginnings of their religion. As for evidence, Stukeley insisted that "a formal and stiff proof of everything...would be odious [hateful] and irksome to the reader," who, if wise, would be convinced without such proof.

This Stukeley is a far cry from the young doctor who made annual excursions to the stone circles and studied them with scientific precision. He was now a middle-aged Anglican minister who referred to himself as "Archdruid." Moreover, Stukeley used the scientific data he had gathered so carefully to support his increasingly fanciful notions about the Druids. The papers he submitted to the antiquarian society, which he had helped found years earlier, were now frequently rejected. According to one acquaintance, Stukeley was "a fanciful man, looked upon as beside himself." In short, he had come to represent the fanciful Druid he had created.

It is thanks to Stukeley that the megaliths on the Wiltshire plain are forever, although incorrectly, linked to the ancient Druids. Today's archaeologists, however, respect Stukeley for his careful investigations and his passion to preserve the ancient monuments, not for his speculations. Moreover, it was Stukeley who first established Stonehenge's orientation toward the sunrise of the summer solstice, a fact which is found in most modern interpretations of the site's original use and meaning. ♜

Stephanie Prescott *is an editor and writer who lives in California.*

William Stukeley believed that Stonehenge traced its origins to the ancient Druids.

THE DRUIDS AT STONEHENGE

The ancient Druids fell victim to the advancing Roman armies and the coming of Christianity. Since the 1700s, however, revived Druidic groups have kept the spirit of the ancient priests alive, especially at Stonehenge, where annual summer solstice celebrations began in the 1800s. In recent years, authorities have begun clamping down on solstice rites and on the caravans of spectators who, drawn by the ritual, camp out for weeks, endangering the monument and its environs. White-robed Druids still gather at Stonehenge to pay homage to the rising sun, but not during the solstice. They do so, however, only with a permit granted by the English Heritage, the organization that oversees the site. Perhaps the problems of recent years will convince today's Druids to return to the sacred groves where, most archaeologists agree, their ancient ancestors really worshipped.

S.P.

IN JUNE OF 1998, FOR THE FIRST TIME IN 20 YEARS, THE DRUIDS WERE ALLOWED TO CONDUCT SUMMER SOLSTICE RITES AT STONEHENGE.

A DATE

ILLUSTRATED BY HEIDI GRAF

WITH AN ARCHAEOLOGIST

by Emily Abbink

Dating ancient artifacts is no simple matter. In fact, there are several dating methods. Which one a scientist uses depends on the properties of the item to be dated and its probable age. One of the most commonly used methods is Carbon 14 or radiocarbon dating, because C14 (as it is called) can date most organic remains such as charcoal, bones, shells, and plants.

An American professor, Willard Libbey, developed C14 dating in 1949. After proving that all living matter contains C14, Libbey stated that when matter dies, the C14 within begins to decay at a known, fixed rate. To

date a dead organic remain, Libbey measured the amount of C14 left in it.

At Stonehenge, archaeologists have measured C14 in recovered charcoal pieces, bones, and broken antler tools, all of which had been mixed with dirt and used to refill the pits dug for the megaliths. Based on the C14 dates, archaeologists determined that there were several building phases.

In recent years, scientists have improved C14 dating with accelerated mass spectrometry (AMS), which is quicker and more accurate. Regular C14 requires large samples, while AMS can date very small artifacts, such as a single seed or a bone splinter. Using this method on Stonehenge artifacts has convinced archaeologists that the site is much older than previously believed. It has also shown that the post holes beneath the parking area were intended originally for wooden building materials more than 8,000 years old.

Another dating method, often used in combination with C14, is tree-ring dating, or dendrochronology (DEN drowe crow NOL eh gee). This technique measures the annual growth rings that most trees produce. These rings are easily seen in a tree trunk's cross-section. Ring thickness varies with weather changes. In dry climates , heavy rains will cause especially thick rings. In mild regions, a sharp cold snap might produce a thinner ring.

Scientists measure and plot these rings to discover patterns of thick and thin

rings. Complete chronological charts are made for various tree species in different regions. By matching the ring patterns with a section of the chart, archaeologists can date such finds as excavated roof beams or posts. Dendrochronology, however, can only date well preserved wood from trees and areas that have been charted.

Because of the lack of uncovered old timbers at Stonehenge, dendrochronology dating has not been used extensively. However, archaeologists have been cross-checking radiocarbon dates using tree-ring dates on bristlecone pines. (This tree is native to the Rocky Mountains and scientists have established tree-ring dates for the bristlecone pine that go back 8,000 years.)

Archaeologists have also worked with other dating methods at Stonehenge. One method involves comparing styles and techniques used at Stonehenge with those used at other sites whose dates are more firmly established. Another surveys the land surface with specially designed electronic equipment that maps, electronically, any underground structures. A third method involves studying the stratigraphy of Stonehenge (that is, the separate layers of land that have accumulated over time) and comparing the results with stratigraphic charts made of other ancient areas. 🏛

Emily Abbink, *the author of* Missions of Monterey Bay, *is an archaeologist who teaches history and anthropology at the University of California Santa Cruz.*

The FOUR

by Sabine Goerke-Shrode

At first glance, Stonehenge appears to be a jumble of 162 stones huddled together on a mound on England's windy Salisbury Plain. Seen from a distance, they appear tiny. Yet, as one nears the Plain, the gray megaliths seem to rise like giants, starkly outlined against the sky — a sight as impressive to today's visitor as it must have been to the ancient worshipper. Sometime around A.D. 500 the Saxons (the early English) named it Stonehenge, meaning a place of "hanging stones." The monument's original name is unknown.

Stonehenge, however, does not date to one time period. Rather, it grew and changed over a period of nearly 2,000 years. What remains today contains elements from every phase of its development. Using various dating techniques, archaeologists have assigned dates to each major phase.

STONEHENGE
Phase 1

Activity began around 4000 B.C., when farmers with herds of cattle settled in the region. They built long mounds flanked by shallow ditches, which they used for buri-

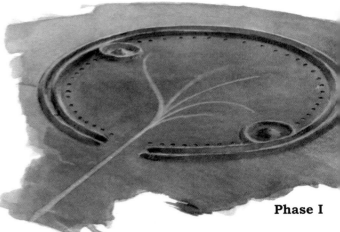

Phase I

als and perhaps as boundary markers. By 3100 B.C., they had built a simple earthenwork enclosure that included a six-foot high circular bank, made of chalk rubble. Within the bank was a circle of 56 evenly spaced round holes, the so-called Aubrey Holes. These holes seem to have been filled in shortly afterward without ever holding anything. Centuries later, many of these holes were reused as burial pits to hold cremated human bones. Why they were dug initially, however, remains a mystery.

While other similar ancient enclosures had a wooden structure in the center, no evidence of one was found at Stonehenge. A group of post holes in the entrance area presents another unsolved puzzle. One theory suggests that they belonged to a wooden entrance structure.

"Great periodicals for research as well as pleasure."

Cobblestone Publishing Company
30 Grove Street, Suite C
Peterborough, NH 03458-1454

III₁₁₁₁₁IIₗ₁ₗₗₗₗₗₗₗₗ₁₁₁₁IIₗₗₗₗₗₗₗₗₗₗₗₗIIₗₗI

HASES *of Stonehenge*

About 85 feet outside the entrance stands the Heel Stone, an untrimmed *sarsen* stone, 16 feet high. It is unclear whether it was quarried locally or dragged 20 miles overland from the Marlborough Downs area. Today the Heel Stone is the only remaining stone from Phase I.

Stonehenge I was used for several hundred years and then abandoned. During that period, other ceremonial monuments such as long earthen avenues, burial mounds, stone and wooden circles, and *henge* enclosures were built nearby, slowly transforming the area into a sacred landscape.

STONEHENGE *Phase 11*

By 2150 B.C., there was much remodeling taking place at Stonehenge. The axis was shifted slightly to the east by widening the entrance. As a result, the structure came to be better aligned with the rising sun at the summer solstice. This shift in alignment seems deliberate and probably had a religious significance.

About 80 bluestones were set up in two circles. These volcanic stones, bluish in color and flecked with pink spots, are found only in the Preseli Mountains in Wales, more than 250 miles away. Why the builders hauled stones weighing about 5 tons each all the way to Stonehenge remains a mystery. Some archaeologists think that blue was sacred color.

A bluestone of exceptional height was erected in the circle's center. Called the Altar Stone today, it may well be the original or a successor. The circles, however, were never completed, and the stones were soon removed and the holes refilled.

Outside the entrance, a ceremonial avenue was constructed, consisting of a parallel pair of banks and ditches run-

> **Sarsen** stones are natural blocks of a sandstone that formed over 70 million years ago. The stone itself is extremely hard.

> A **henge** is a circular, man-made mound of earth that has an outer bank and an inner ditch broken by one or two entrances.

Phase II

ning for about 500 yards. The stones flanking the old entrance were reset on a line between the entrance and the Heel Stone.

Around this time, the Station Stones appear inside the bank. These are four roughly finished sarsen stones, two of them surrounded by small ditches. They form a rectangle in alignment with the new axis. Whether they belong in Phase II or date to a later time remains uncertain.

STONEHENGE
Phase IIIa

The most significant building period at Stonehenge began around 2100 B.C. At the time, there was a shift in population from small, self-governing villages to communities ruled by powerful and wealthy chieftains. This change brought more people together under one ruler and made the ambitious building program of Phase IIIa possible.

In the years that followed, workers dragged 10 great sarsen stones from Marlborough Downs, trimmed them, and then set them up in a horseshoe formation, with the opening facing the northeast. Each of the five pairs, their size increasing from 20 to 24 feet, was topped with a lintel to form a *trilithon.* Today, only three trilithons remain standing.

Thirty smaller sarsen stones, each about 16 feet

Trilithon is a Greek word meaning "three stones."

Phase IIIa

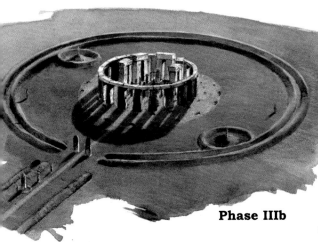

Phase IIIb

Around 2000 B.C. 20 of the original bluestones, each six to eight feet high, were dressed (that is, smoothed) and set within the sarsen horseshoe.

Around 1550 B.C., two circles of holes (the so-called Y and Z holes) were dug outside the sarsen circle to hold bluestones. These circles were never completed, nor were the stones ever set.

STONEHENGE
Phase IIIc

Not long after, the bluestones were reset again. The result was a bluestone circle within the sarsen circle and a bluestone horseshoe within the sarsen horseshoe. Set at the center of both horseshoes is the Altar Stone, so named by early excavators who found it on the ground and believed it to be an altar.

Phase IIIc

high and square in shape, were set around the trilithons in a circle about 100 feet in diameter. These stones supported a continuous ring of massive stone lintels. Two upright stones were set in the entrance way. One of these is the so-called Slaughter Stone, a roughly dressed 21-foot high sarsen. It was so named because early explorers thought its rough surface was ideal to catch blood offerings from sacrifices.

Stonehenge IIIa was the end of the main building period and the use of sarsen stone. The precision with which the complex was laid out, and the architectural details it displays, are unparalleled in other such structures of northwestern Europe.

ILLUSTRATED BY RICHARD SCHLECHT

19

STONEHENGE
Phase IV

Around 1100 B.C., the Avenue was extended for one and a half miles to reach the Avon River. This was the final phase in Stonehenge's development.

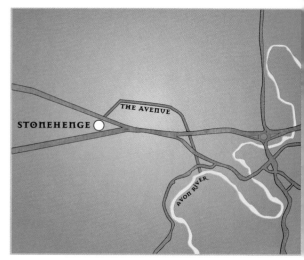

Phase IV

Sabine Goerke-Shrode, a classical archaeologist, is the Curator of Collections at the Vacaville Museum in California.

The Four Phases of Stonehenge

STONEHENGE I	**C. 3100 – 2300 B.C.**
STONEHENGE II	**C. 2150 – C. 2000 B.C.**
STONEHENGE IIIA	**C. 2100 – C. 2000 B.C.**
STONEHENGE IIIB	**C. 2000 – C. 1550 B.C.**
STONEHENGE IIIC	**C. 1550 – C. 1100 B.C.**
STONEHENGE IV	**C. 1100 B.C.**

The abbreviation **c.** stands for the Latin preposition *circa*, meaning "about" or "around."

LET'S TAKE A CLOSER LOOK

By Emily Abbink

Stonehenge's dark, gigantic stones loom eerily above windswept, grass-covered plains, and can be seen for miles around. Over the centuries, many stones have toppled and cracked or disappeared — a fact that seems to have increased the sense of mystery and isolation. Fewer than half the stones stand as originally placed. Very possibly there were wooden structures too, now long rotted away.

From the air, it is easy to see that Stonehenge is a series of *concentric,* circular earth and stone structures. Built by different peoples at different times, the oldest sections that are still visible generally form the outside

Concentric means having a center in common.

Originally, stone lintels connected this large, upright stone to other similar stones. To lock the giant blocks together, workers shaped a knob-like piece that would stick out above the top of the upright stone (see circled area above). They then set the "knob" inside the mortise hole they had cut into the lintel that was to be positioned above it.

A **lintel** is the horizontal crosspiece over a door or window.

perimeter. The later sections are those found within the perimeter.

To make the broad circular ditch that was dug into the chalk bedrock during Phase I, the builders used deer antler picks. The loose fill from the ditch was then piled up to make an earthen mound about 320 feet in diameter. This mound lay just inside the ditch and was once over six feet tall. Today, it has weathered to about two feet. Both the ditch and the embankment are broken by a 35-foot entrance way to the northeast.

Before positioning the stones during the Phase IIIa construction period, workers tapered one end of each stone and then, at this end, carved a protruding tenon (a part that projects at the end of a piece of stone or wood). They then shaped sandstone *lintel* segments with overlapping ends and mortise holes. The lintels were hoisted up and positioned atop the uprights with each mortise hole fitting over a tenon. In this way, the lintels formed a continuous, interlocking ring above the sandstones.

During Phase IIIb, builders erected a horseshoe of sarsen trilithons. Each was a free-standing structure consisting of two massive uprights that were even larger than those in the outer circle. A single sandstone lintel crowned each of the five pairs of uprights. Opening to the northeast, this horseshoe formation was aligned with the entrance way, the Heel Stone, and the Avenue. 🏛

Even the smaller stones at Stonehenge dwarf human visitors to the site. Here, a woman leans against a bluestone that once formed part of the outer bluestone circle. Behind it stands one of the five sarsen trilithons, still upright and still in its original position. This photo was taken in the 1960's when visitors were able to walk about Stonehenge.

The
World of
Stonehenge

Atlantic Ocean

SCANDINAVIA

DENMARK

GERMANY

EUROPE

ENGLAND

BRITTANY

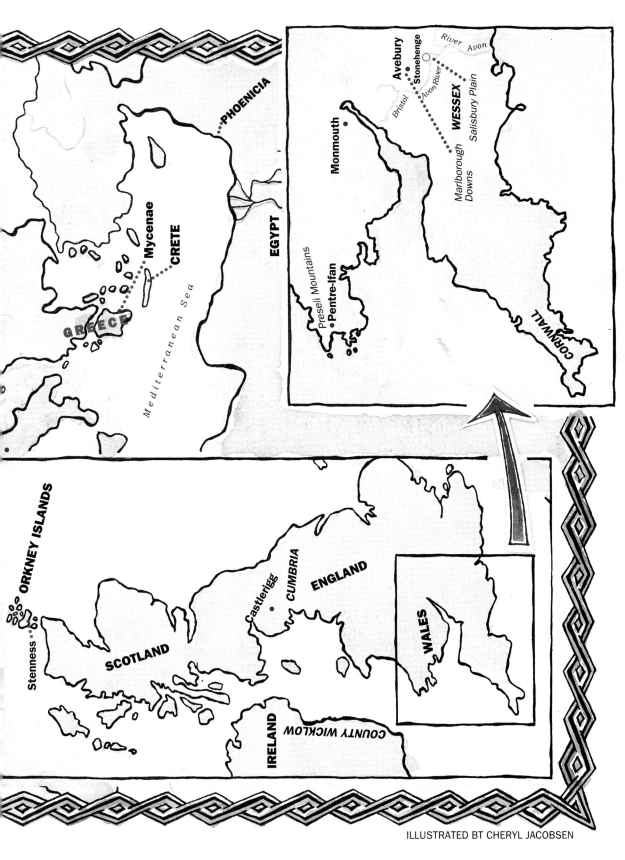

ILLUSTRATED BT CHERYL JACOBSEN

by Betsy F. Ryan

Although the exact reasons why Stonehenge was built remain a mystery, many believe that the massive stones and the sun were used together to gather information. Through the centuries and for many cultures, the sun has provided a very important piece of information — the time of day. A simple way to read "sun time" is to use a sundial.

As the sun moves across the sky, it casts a shadow that can be interpreted to tell the hour of the day. The piece used to cast a shadow on a sundial is called a gnomon.

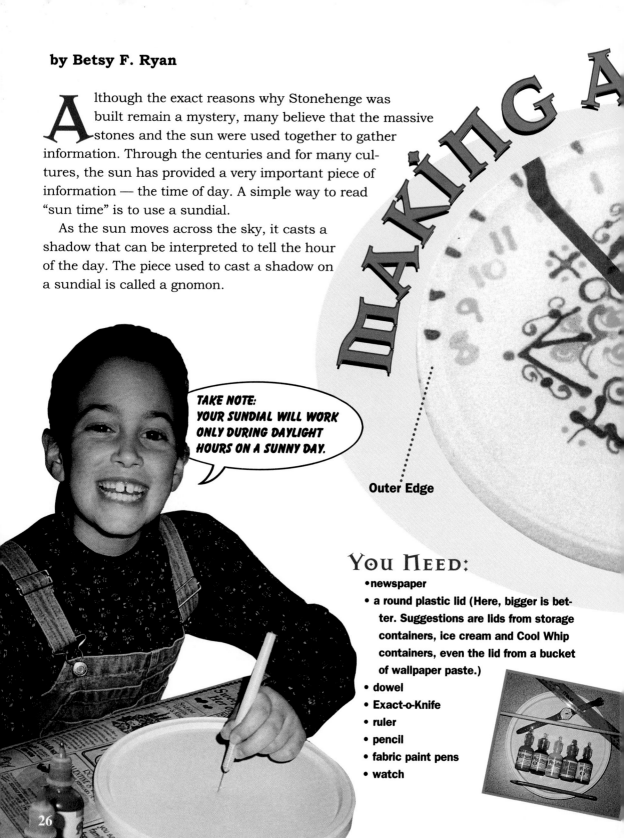

MAKING A

TAKE NOTE:
YOUR SUNDIAL WILL WORK
ONLY DURING DAYLIGHT
HOURS ON A SUNNY DAY.

Outer Edge

You Need:

- newspaper
- a round plastic lid (Here, bigger is better. Suggestions are lids from storage containers, ice cream and Cool Whip containers, even the lid from a bucket of wallpaper paste.)
- dowel
- Exact-o-Knife
- ruler
- pencil
- fabric paint pens
- watch

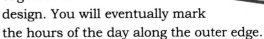
········· **Gnomon**

SUNDIAL

TO MAKE YOUR SUNDIAL

1 Lay out the newspaper on your work space.

2 Find the center of your lid and, using a ruler, measure the length from top to bottom. Mark the middle with your pencil.

3 **With adult supervision,** cut an "X" over the pencil marking. NOTE: The X needs to be big enough to slide the dowel through it.

4 Using fabric paint pens, draw a design on your lid. Be sure to leave the outer edge free of design. You will eventually mark the hours of the day along the outer edge.

5 On a sunny day, hold a watch in your hand and turn it so the hour hand points to the sun. Holding the watch very still, find the spot exactly between the hour hand and 12. This is south. North is in the opposite direction.

6 Stick the dowel — your gnomon — into the ground.

7 Slide the plastic lid into the dowel.

8 Starting early in the morning and then every daylight hour thereafter, mark where the shadow falls on the outer edge of the plastic lid with your fabric paint pens. Do this at 6:00, 7:00, 8:00, etc. — right through until evening.

You now have a sundial you can leave outside no matter what the weather is, and it will tell you what the time is on sunny days. If you move your sundial, you will have to mark again where the shadows fall.

Betsy F. Ryan *has her Masters Degree in Art Education and presently resides in Albany, New York, with her family.*

THE BUILDING OF STONEHENGE

by Janeen R. Adil

Did Merlin, the mighty magician of the legendary King Arthur's court, erect Stonehenge? Or was it the work of the devil himself? Perhaps Roman builders or Mediterranean seafarers set the huge stones into place. Or was Stonehenge the result of natural forces?

Over the centuries, stories and legends have "explained" how Stonehenge was built. While many mysteries still surround the construction, archaeologists have formed likely theories as to how the ancient Britons actually erected the massive stones.

We know that Stonehenge's bluestones came from the Preseli Mountains in southern Wales. To get them to Salisbury Plain, it is thought, the stones were placed on a sort of sled with wooden runners, which was rolled over a long line of logs. The last log would be picked up and placed in front of the sled. For 16 miles

this process was repeated over and over, until the stones reached the sea.

There the stones were loaded onto rafts made by lashing small canoes together. Some scientists believe that the bluestones were floated around England's southwestern peninsula to Stonehenge. Others believe that a shorter route was followed, along the Bristol Avon River and then across land. Archaeologists in the 1950s successfully duplicated these roller-raft methods, although they stopped short of trying the rafts in deep, open water.

The huge sarsen stones came from Marlborough Downs, about 20 miles from Stonehenge. They may also have been moved to the site with rollers and rafts. Some scientists, however, think it is more likely that the sarsen stones were moved on some type of sled. This could have been done in winter, when ice and snow made the going somewhat easier.

Other researchers suggest that a wooden trackway could have been built along the route. An experiment conducted in 1995 involved a stone equivalent to one of the largest trilithons. Earlier estimates had been that some 500 people were required to move one stone. However, by using just a greased wooden trackway and

ropes, only about 100 people were needed to pull the stone along!

Once the sarsens reached the site, an enormous amount of labor went into shaping them. One method may have involved driving wooden wedges into cracks in the stones. To chip away excess stone, the early Britons used the simplest of tools: rounded chunks of sarsen. After this initial shaping, the builders went on to give some of the sarsens a final polish. Pulling a larger piece of sarsen back and forth over the surface would have helped them grind down rough spots.

Before raising a sarsen upright, its bottom was shaped to a dull point. Then, with antler and bone tools, the builders

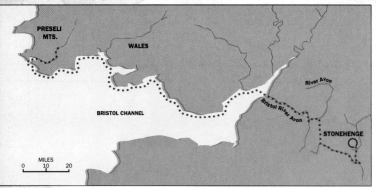

To raise the huge lintels into place, the builders may have built long earthen ramps extending from the base of the two upright sarsens. The lintel could then have been dragged up the ramp and so maneuvered into place. Many archaeologists, however, believe that a platform of logs was built next to or surrounding the vertical stones. As one end of the lintel was raised with levers, more logs were added under it and, in this way, the lintel was lifted to the proper height. 🏛

dug a hole, one side of which was at a 45-degree angle. Next they tipped the sarsen into the hole and slid it down the angled side. Pulling the sarsen vertical with ropes required the efforts of perhaps 350 people. Or, as recent experiments show, it could have been done with only 75 or so workers using ropes and an A-frame of logs behind the stone for leverage. Finally, the hole was packed with dirt, rocks, bones, and old tools.

Janeen R. Adil, *a regular contributor to* CALLIOPE, *lives with her family in Quakertown, Pennsylvania.*

In a 1954 experiment, English schoolboys, using a raft that Stonehenge's builders could easily have made, moved a concrete replica of a bluestone down the River Avon to Stonehenge.

Cobblestone Publishing Company
30 Grove Street, Suite C
Peterborough, NH 03458-1454

IIl.....II.l..l.l.l.l.l..l.....IIl.l..l.l.l.l..l..l.l.IIl.l

The WESSEX CHIEFTAINS:
BUILDERS OF STONEHENGE?

by Diana Childress

In September of 1808, a group of men cut into Bush Barrow, a large burial mound within sight of Stonehenge, and struck gold. At the center of the barrow, near the skeleton of a large man, lay bronze and copper daggers, a bronze ax, and a large belt buckle and a breast plate of finely wrought gold. Thousands of tiny gold pins embellished a wooden dagger handle. Its craftsmanship "could not be surpassed (if indeed equaled) by the most able workman of modern times," wrote Sir Richard Colt Hoare in describing the findings.

Bush Barrow contained the richest grave goods known from prehistoric Britain, but it is not unique. In exca-

vating other round barrows of the late Neolithic and early Bronze Age (c. 2500 to 1600 B.C.) in the vicinity of Stonehenge, archaeologists unearthed more gold ornaments, beads of *faience* and amber, bronze tools and weapons, and a variety of pottery. Unlike earlier Neolithic "long barrow" graves that held the bones of many people, round barrows marked single burials of apparently wealthy, important individuals.

Faience is baked clay that has been decorated with colored glazes which are not transparent or translucent.

The new form of burial represents a social change that archaeologists call "Wessex culture." Wessex refers to a natural geographic region of chalk plains that includes most of the modern counties of Wiltshire and Dorset. Around 2500 B.C., the area became more settled. Farmers grew surplus crops and had time to work on construction projects during slack periods of the agricultural year. Wessex culture graves, with their state-of-the-art weapons and flashy accessories, suggest that warrior chieftains ruled this society.

The Wessex region — and Stonehenge in particular — lay at the crossroads of several ancient trackways. In earlier times, traders carried stone tools and pottery (and doubtless other, more perishable goods) from one end of England to the other. Similar goods probably also traveled by sea along the English coast and up the River Avon. The luxury articles in the round barrows, however, tapped new, overseas markets. The gold most likely originated

in County Wicklow in Ireland. The bronze work shares features with artifacts from Brittany and southern Germany. Archaeologists believe the amber came from Scandinavia. The blue faience beads, perhaps the most exotic items from the round barrows, may have been manufactured in Egypt.

On the theory that Wessex trade reached the Mediterranean, archaeologists once thought that the civilizations of Mycenaean Greece and Minoan Crete influenced the building of Stonehenge. Daggers and axes found in Wessex graves and carved on the sarsens at Stonehenge resemble those from Mycenae and Crete, and the Greeks traded in Egyptian faience (a shiny blue-green glazed synthetic material). Recent radiocarbon dates, however, show that Stonehenge predates the flowering of those early Mediterranean cultures.

Whether or not Wessex rulers traded directly with Mycenae and Crete, they played some role in the commercial networks that crisscrossed northern Europe. Mines in southwestern England known as Cornwall gave Wessex access to tin, an essential and relatively scarce ingredient of bronze, which was

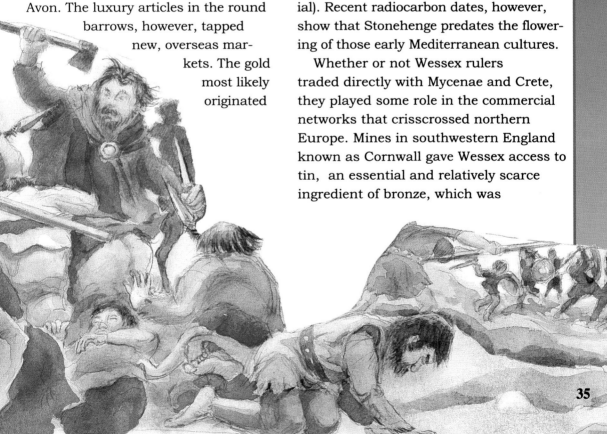

at that time the material of choice for tools and weapons throughout Europe. Historians believe that the Wessex chieftains might have amassed their fortunes by controlling the production of Cornish tin. Yet, whatever the source of the tin, their wealth lasted several centuries.

The most intriguing question about their culture is its relationship to Stonehenge. Several centuries of strong, wealthy rulers could provide the leadership and organization needed for such a difficult, long-term project as Stonehenge. Although we lack firm dates to pinpoint both the beginning and the end of Wessex culture, archaeologists agree that Stonehenge was still undergoing alterations during the late Wessex period. Did the Wessex Chieftains design and build the great sarsen circle? It may be possible. Viewing the impressive finds from Bush Barrow, archaeologist Julian Richards speculates: "Perhaps we are looking into the burial of the person who revived Stonehenge, the architect, the sponsor, buried in his finery and overlooking his lasting monument."

Diana Childress is *a freelance writer who spent the first part of 1998 in England while her husband was on sabbatical at the University of Exeter.*

Finds in the burial mound at Bush Barrow have helped archaeologists better understand the life and customs of the early Britons.

FROM PAST TO PRESENT
STONEHENGE GOES PUBLIC

by Diana Childress

BY THE EARLY 1800S, STONEHENGE ATTRACTED SO MANY TOURISTS THAT THE OWNERS HIRED GUARDS TO KEEP THE CROWDS FROM CHOPPING OFF PIECES OF STONE TO CARRY HOME AS SOUVENIRS. MANY PEOPLE ARGUED THAT STONEHENGE AND OTHER ANCIENT MONUMENTS SHOULD BECOME PUBLIC

ILLUSTRATED BY BRUCE DODGE

37

property, protected and managed by the British government, but landowners opposed the idea.

About 4,000 years had past since the last bluestone eased into its slot in the horseshoe at the center of Stonehenge, completing the monument as we know it. Construction, however, had not stopped. During the next 500 years, workers dug two rings of rectangular holes outside the great sarsen circle. These holes, which were never filled, were apparently the last alterations to the monument made by the Wessex chieftains, whose rich burials also came to an end around the same time. Work on Stonehenge was over.

People had still visited and used the great monument in the centuries that followed, but it was no longer the main focus of ritual activity for the region. Whether the ancient Druids worshipped there when the Celts came to Britain after 600 B.C. or the Romans tried to tear the monument down are both unknowns. No written mention of Stonehenge survives from Roman or Saxon times. Only in the 1100s does Stonehenge enter the historical record: "No one can conceive how such great stones have been so raised aloft, or why they were built there" wrote a historian in 1130. More imaginative writers attributed the building of Stonehenge to giants. Geoffrey of Monmouth, writing in 1136, asserts that Merlin magically transported this "Giant's Ring" from Ireland as a memorial to British lords massacred by the invading Saxons in the late 400s.

Recognizing the national importance of Stonehenge, King James I sent the renowned architect Inigo Jones to examine the site in the early 1600s. King Charles II also took a personal interest, and visited Stonehenge with John Aubrey, the discoverer of the so-called Aubrey holes. The land on which Stonehenge was built was, during these time periods, in private hands. It had changed ownership from time to time and had, at one point, belonged to Sir Lawrence Washington, an ancestor of the first President of the United States, for about 50 years.

Sir Edmund Antrobus, who purchased Stonehenge in 1824, refused access to government inspectors and archaeologists. The need for better care of the monument became obvious in 1900 when a severe gale toppled one of the sarsen stones and its lintel. The Antrobus family responded by fencing in the property and allowing a police constable to supervise the area and an engineer to stabilize the stones.

Stonehenge finally became public property through the generosity of Cecil Chubb, who bought the monument when the Antrobus estate was auctioned in 1915. Chubb gave it to the nation three years later. By then, roads, an airfield, and houses cluttered the landscape. In 1929, in response to a national appeal, the government purchased 1500 acres to restore and preserve open space around Stonehenge. Many modern structures were demolished, but the huge numbers of visitors necessitated the addition of parking facilities and a visitors' center in 1968.

Several repairs have also been made: The stones that fell in 1797, 1900, and 1963 have been raised and concrete has been used to fix several of the sarsens more firmly in their sockets. While some people had hoped that the monument would be restored with new stones, a more conservative approach prevailed.

In the future, English Heritage, the organization that oversees the site, envisions moving tourist facilities farther away and sending the roaring traffic on nearby roads into tunnels. By eliminating all modern interference and extending the grassy parkland around it, English Heritage hopes to enhance our experience of visiting Stonehenge and to deepen our understanding of it.

MONOLITHIC REFRESHMENT

TEA
LEMONADE
CAKES

SCONES
PUNCH
CHEESE

A World Heritag

I n 1986, the World Heritage Committee selected Stonehenge as a World Heritage Site. As such, it joins a diverse group of places valued for their uniqueness. Some, like Stonehenge, the Maya temples in Mexico, and the Egyptian pyramids, tell stories of ancient peoples. Others, like the Statue of Liberty and the Citadel of Haiti, which was built by slaves who had gained their freedom, symbolize human hope. Still others, like the Grand Canyon and the Carlsbad Caverns in New Mexico, reflect billions of years of the earth's history.

The World Heritage list grew out of a concern that modern life threatened the survival of these irreplaceable treasures. To protect and preserve them, the General Conference of UNESCO (United Nations Educational, Scientific, and Cultural Organization) in

Site

1972 adopted an agreement signed by 145 countries. It established the World Heritage Committee, which chooses the places to be included and arranges for technical advice and financial aid for any places that are in danger of destruction. The agreement also established the World Heritage Center, which sees that each member country protects sites within its territory. Through international cooperation, World Heritage hopes to preserve the natural, cultural, and historical legacies of all humanity.

D.C.

The size and mystery surrounding Stonehenge have inspired countless artists through the centuries. In this 1835 painting, John Constable used a wildly dramatic sky as the backdrop for the once great circle that he depicted as a proud, yet fallen mass of ruins.

WORKING WITH STONES

by Betsy F. Ryan

When looking at Stonehenge, whether in a picture or on site, you are overcome by a tremendous sense of wonder. How, you may ask, was this done? How were these stones moved and lifted into place? Stones are very difficult objects with which to work: to change their shapes and textures is a challenging task. To help you understand what an awesome accomplishment Stonehenge is, try working with some stones yourself. Your goal with this project is to build a sculpture using as many stones as you wish. As you search for stones that appeal to you, examine each closely and you will begin to see something that you want the stones to become. This is very much like watching clouds in the sky and seeing their shapes become different objects. Now, let your imagination take over and have fun!

YOU NEED:

- **cardboard**
- **scissors**
- **stones**
- **hot glue gun**
- **acrylic paints**
- **brushes**
- **water**
- **newspaper**
- **optional items: paper, buttons, fabric scraps, etc.**

TO MAKE A ROCK SCULPTURE

1 Search your neighborhood for stones that appeal to you. You will probably want to collect lots of them so that you can explore different ideas.

2 Lay out newspaper for your work area.

3 After examining the stones closely, determine how you want to put them together to create your sculpture. (It helps to limit the number of stones that you use.) Begin first with a large stone; then, add others as you wish.

4 Cut a piece of cardboard to use as your base. The size depends on how large you want your sculpture to be.

5 Using the cardboard as a secure and sturdy base, start creating your sculpture. With a glue gun, attach any stones that need to be joined together.

6 Use your imagination and continue working on the sculpture with your paint, brushes, water, optional items, and glue gun. Remember to allow time after each step for drying and setting in place before you add more stones.

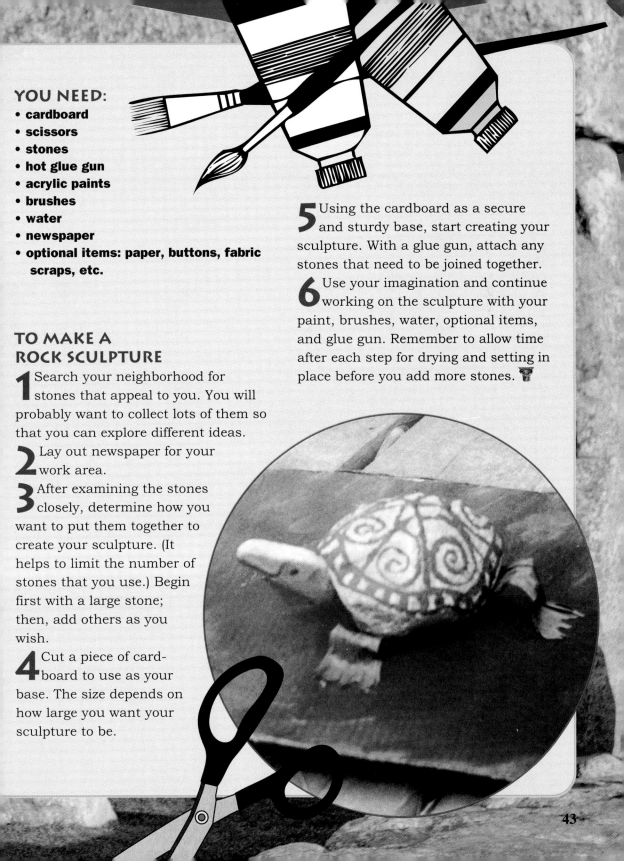

Fun With Words

WORD ORIGINS
MEGALITH

Like "monolith" and "neolithic," the word "megalith" traces its origin to the root word *lithos*, Greek for "stone." Speakers of English merely added a variety of prefixes to form words that refer to a specific type of stone or to people who work with stone. Thus, megalith (*megas* is Greek for "great") denotes "a huge stone." Monolith (*monos* is Greek for "single") denotes "a single large stone block." Neolithic (*neos* is Greek for "new") refers to that ancient period of time when people first used polished stone tools.

WORD STORIES
FOSSIL

The ancient Romans thought it quite appropriate to use the verbal participle *fossus*, meaning "dug up," to form the noun *fossa*, meaning "ditch." Centuries later, speakers of English considered it just as appropriate to borrow *fossa*, change it to "fossil," and use it to refer to anything that was dug up out of the ground. In time, the meaning narrowed, and today a "fossil" refers to the hardened remains of ancient plant or animal life.

TRAVEL

Would you ever guess that the words "travel" and "travail" both trace their roots to the Latin words *tres* and *palus*, meaning "three" and "stick"? In the Middle Ages, the French had an instrument used to torture people that was composed of three pieces of wood. To name this device, the French borrowed the two Latin words and formed *tripalium*. As the years passed, French modified *trepalium* to *travailler* and used it as a verb meaning " to work hard." Speakers of English borrowed the French *travailler*, changed the spelling to "travail" but left the meaning the same. English also used "travail" to mean "going from one

place to another." The word certainly seemed appropriate enough since journeys at this time were quite difficult — roads were not paved and the threat of an attack by bandits or wild beasts was always a possibility. Gradually, two English words developed, the old "travail," meaning hard work and the new "travel," meaning a journey.

EXPRESSIONS
"TO BE UNSTRUNG"

The invention of the bow and arrow predates historical records. Thus, no documents or inscriptions exist that tell us by whom or when this weapon was first used. Through the years, advances in technology have helped archers make improvements in its design. During the Middle Ages, one such improvement involved the wood used to fashion a bow. At the time, English archers found that by using the yew — an evergreen shrub — they could make a bow that stood as tall as the archer himself. In addition, this bow had enough power to send an arrow 100 yards and have its point enter an oak tree (one of the hardest woods known) to the depth of one inch.

Unfortunately, this bow had one major disadvantage. When not in use, this bow could not be kept strung, since the constant tension weakened the wood and, in time, prevented the bow from bending

properly. For this reason, archers found it necessary to loosen one end of the bowstring on their yew bows when they were not using them. Naturally, this placed the archer at a distinct disadvantage, because a yew bow required time to restring and no enemy would grant his opponent that time. This was a fearsome prospect and gave rise to the expression "to be unstrung." At first, it referred to a nervous archer with a loosened bowstring. In more recent times, it has been used to refer to anyone who feels extremely uneasy or fearful.

ILLUSTRATED BY TOM LOPES

BOOKS

Bip Quiz: Great Civilizations (New York: Sterling Publishing, 1996) includes 100 questions and answers on topics ranging from the pyramids of Egypt to the Coliseum in Rome to the stone walls of Zimbabwe. When you press the "BipPen" to the black shape next to what you think is the right answer, a green flashing light and a "beep" lets you know you're correct. A flashing red light and an "errp" sound announces that you're incorrect. Other books in the series include: *Countries of the World, Great Dates in History, Great Discoveries, Great Inventions,* and *Famous People.*

Encyclopedia of Word and Phrase Origins by Robert Hendrickson (New York: Facts On File, 1997) traces the fascinating origins and development of more than 9,000 words and phrases from A to Zzz, including slang, proverbs, animal and plant names, place-names, nicknames, historical expressions, foreign-language expressions, and phrases from literature. Clear and easy-to-read, it provides a wealth of background material for anyone interested in words and language.

Mysterious Places: The Master Builders (New York: Chelsea House, 1994) focuses on 10 ancient sites, including Stonehenge,

Catal Hüyük, Troy, Chichen Itza, and Machu Picchu, and the people who built them. Maps and clear, informative illustrations enhance the text.

Seven Mysterious Wonders of the World by Celia King (San Francisco, California: Chronicle Books, 1993) includes clever, miniature pop-ups of Stonehenge, Easter Island, the Nasca Lines, Atlantis, the Egyptian "Labyrinth," Shangri-La, and the Bermuda Triangle. Each site is accompanied by a brief, but informative text.

Stonehenge by Wendy Mass (San Diego, California: Lucent Books, 1998) presents a detailed introduction to this megalithic monument through the ages. Chapter headings include: "Early Stages of Construction," "What was the Purpose of Stonehenge?", and "Destruction, Restoration, and Preservation." A time-line prefaces the text and a great variety of photos and diagrams enhances the reader's understanding of this World Heritage Site.

Stonehenge Revealed by David Souden (New York: Facts on File, 1997) includes seven chapters: "Understanding Stonehenge," "The Stonehenge Landscape," "Stonehenge and Prehistory," "The Making of the Megaliths," "The People of Stonehenge," "Ritual and the Heavens," and "The

Legacy of Stonehenge." Numerous photos, charts, diagrams, and maps accompany this excellent, well-researched and well-written text.

Stones and Bones! How Archaeologists Trace Human Origins prepared by the Geography Department (Minneapolis, Minnesota: Runestone Press, 1994) explains the importance and significance of ancient finds, such as rock paintings by Australian Aborigines and "Lucy's" remains, as well as the work done, past and present, by paleontologists around the world.

The Young Oxford Book of Archaeology by Norah Moloney (New York: Oxford University Press, 1995) uses photographs, detailed reconstructions, and maps to complement a well-researched and very interesting-to-read text that examines and interprets evidence from several fascinating archaeological sites. Feature articles cover topics such as Stonehenge, Mohenjodaro, Deir-el-Medineh, Tenochtitlán, rock art, Sutton Hoo, and the Nunamiut of Alaska.

VIDEOS

Stonehenge, one of a five-hour, five-part set titled "Secrets of Lost Empires," in the NOVA mini-series. For more information call: 1-800-255-9424.

REFERENCE

Stonehenge Decoded by Gerald S. Hawkins (New York: Doubleday and Company, 1965) is considered a key text on the theories and interpretations of this ancient site.

The Stonehenge People: An Exploration of Life in Neolithic Britain 4700-2000 B.C. by Rodney Castleden (New York: Routledge & Kegan Paul, 1987) includes four main sections: Settlement and Agriculture; Industry, Technology and Communications; The Ceremonial Monuments; and People, Polity, and Philosophy.

ALSO RECOMMENDED

Opposing Viewpoints - Great Mysteries Series: Stonehenge by Peter & Connie Roop (San Diego, California: Greenhaven Press, 1989)

The Reference Guide to Famous Engineering Landmarks of the World by Lawrence H. Berlow (Phoenix, Arizona: The Oryx Press, 1998)

Science and Stonehenge by Barry Cunliffe and Colin Renfrew (New York: Oxford University Press, 1997)

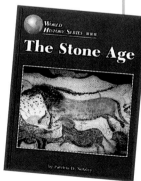

World Political Maps, as well as a great variety of Early European History Maps, all clearly marked and easy to understand (Indianapolis, Indiana: George F. Cram Co.)

World History Series: The Stone Age by Patricia D. Netzley (San Diego, California: Lucent Books, 1998)

Calliope's World

Russia

Russia, a proof that commu-
   nism doesn't work,
Former symbols of communist
   power lying in the streets
   crumbling,
Elderly with stick brooms sweeping blossoms
   that fall like snow,
Vendors in the street selling past memories of
   Soviet aggression,
Crime running rampant, organzied mafia tak-
   ing charge,
Shops unlit, a different place,
Sadness and disparity in the people's eyes,
A glimmer of hope, left only in the minds of
   children.

Chris Guska
Bay Village, Ohio

Summertime

Going to the beach,
Swimming in the ocean
Feeling the seaweed tickle your toes
Collecting seashells
Getting a tan in the shimmering sun
Building sandcastles with seaweed walls
Feeling the sand go between your toes
Having a picnic lunch
Packing up and readying to go.

Eloise Ntekim
Queens, New York

Russia

The flowers dance in the sunlight like the birds
   with red, orange, and green breasts soaring
   through the sky, like the mountains rising
   higher, higher, every time the wind whistles
   in my ears like the valley skipping forever...

This is the land of the poor.
   This is the land that is beautiful
   This is the land I love...
         This is Russia.

Mira Kohl
Wellesley, Massachusetts

My Old Bike

My old bike, I got from dad,
Is not the best I've ever had.
The chain jumps off.
The gears don't work.
Its steering shakes
With twisty jerks.
The brakes don't stop.
The pedals squeak.
An hour's ride
Would take a week.
The tires are bald.
The spokes are bent.
When I start to go,
It's already gone.
The horn doesn't work.
The lights are dim.
Even in gravel,
The wheels won't spin!
The paint's rubbed off.
The chrome doesn't shine.
The seats are not soft.
But I don't mind,
Because my dad got it for me,
Although he probably got it for free.
It gets me where I want to go,
Even if it's rather slow.

Jamie E. Young
Poplar Bluff, Missouri

Wolf Creek

Baskets made of straw
pine needles and bark
Deer skins being
brain washed
and scraped
Clay being
molded
into wonderous pottery
Young men chipping and
carving arrowheads of stone
The twisting and braiding of sinew
corn husks, rafia, and grasses by the
river create cortage, the rope
Creek bed filled with
visions of the past
Wolf Creek

Brandi Gilpin
Bluefield, West Virginia